The 1963 March on Washington

Speeches and Songs for Civil Rights

Jake Miller

The Rosen Publishing Group's

PowerKids Press™

New York

Published in 2004 by The Rosen Publishing Group, Inc.
29 East 21st Street, New York, NY 10010

First Edition

Editor: Frances E. Ruffin
Book Design: Emily Muschinske

Photo Credits: Cover and title page © Hulton-Deutsch Collection/CORBIS; pp. 5 (left), 12, 19, 20, 22 © Flip Shulke/CORBIS; pp. 5 (right), 19 (inset) © Wally McNamee/CORBIS; p. 6 © Donald Uhrbrock/TimePix; pp. 6 (inset), 8, 14, 15, 16 © Bettmann/CORBIS; p. 11 © Library of Congress, Prints and Photographs Division.

Miller, Jake, 1969–
The 1963 March on Washington : speeches and songs for civil rights / Jake Miller.— 1st ed.
    p. cm. — (The library of the civil rights movement)
Includes bibliographical references (p.) and index.
  ISBN 0-8239-6255-5 (library binding)
1. March on Washington for Jobs and Freedom, Washington, D.C., 1963—Juvenile literature. 2. Civil rights demonstrations—Washington (D.C.)—History—20th century—Juvenile literature. 3. African Americans—Civil rights—History—20th century—Juvenile literature. [1. March on Washington for Jobs and Freedom, Washington, D.C., 1963. 2. Civil rights demonstrations. 3. African Americans—Civil rights.] I. Title.
  F200 .M55 2003
  323.1'196073'09046—dc21
                                                                        2001007245

Manufactured in the United States of America

Contents

Coming to Washington

On August 27, 1963, a group of carpenters were hammering the last nails into a platform on the steps of the Lincoln Memorial, a statue in Washington, D.C., that honors President Abraham Lincoln. They were getting ready for the March on Washington for Jobs and Freedom. Thousands of people were on their way to the nation's capital. They were planning to march to the park in front of the memorial, known as the Washington Mall. The march was scheduled for the next day, but people were already beginning to arrive. Most of the visitors were black, but some of them were white. They were coming from all over the country. They were coming to let the government and the nation know that they wanted equal treatment for all American citizens, black and white.

More than 250,000 people came to the March on Washington. Left: Many people brought their families. Right: People traveled to Washington, D.C., from many cities and states, and even from other countries.

Then and Now

During the 1950s and 1960s, thousands of people, black and white, took to the streets to protest what some called the absence of democracy. By the late 1960s, Congress began to pass laws that were fair for all U.S. citizens.

The **PRESENCE OF SEGREGATION** Is **THE ABSENCE OF DEMOCRACY** **JIM CROW MUST GO!**

The Civil Rights Movement

Early in the twentieth century, the **Civil Rights movement** got underway to end **Jim Crow laws**. These laws were created by southern states in the late 1800s to keep people of different races apart by **segregation**. Black children were not allowed to go to the same schools as white children. Blacks and whites could not even sit next to one another in restaurants, in theaters, or even on buses. In many places, blacks were not allowed to vote. Civil rights leaders went to court to fight Jim Crow laws. They organized **boycotts** and **protests** against bus companies and other businesses. By 1963, there were civil rights **demonstrations** across the country. Often white **racists** responded to these peaceful protests with violence. Many civil rights supporters were sent to jail. Some were hurt, and some were killed.

Freedom rides (inset) and boycotting businesses were two ways that civil rights workers hoped to get rid of segregation. As the burning bus shows, sometimes these demonstrations became dangerous.

An Old Idea

For many years people talked about having a huge march in Washington, D.C. In 1941, during World War II (1939–1945), blacks could not get jobs in the **defense industries**. A. Philip Randolph, president of a **labor union** for black railroad workers, wanted to lead a march to make jobs available to black people. He wanted President Franklin D. Roosevelt to force businesses to integrate black workers. Before the march happened, Roosevelt heard about the idea for the march and ordered that blacks be hired for defense jobs. In 1963, Randolph brought back the idea of a march. He met with leaders of many civil rights groups. Dr. Martin Luther King Jr. had become a great leader in the Civil Rights movement. He signed on early to help lead the march. The march grew to include many thousands of marchers.

A. Philip Randolph organized the March on Washington in 1963. Earlier Randolph had helped to convince President Harry Truman to eliminate segregation in the military.

Jobs and Freedom

In 1963, black people were often paid less than white people for the same work. They were also more likely than whites not to have a job at all. A. Philip Randolph was mostly interested in helping blacks to get better jobs. He wanted job training for blacks and an increase in the **minimum wage**. Many of the other leaders of the march on Washington, D.C., were more interested in getting blacks more freedom from unfair laws. They wanted to end segregation in schools and housing. They hoped that the march would meet both goals. John F. Kennedy, who was the president of the United States at that time, had just announced plans for a new set of civil rights laws. The leaders thought the march would be a good way to make sure that Congress passed these laws.

The national headquarters for the organizers of the March on Washington had a banner announcing the March on Washington for Jobs and Freedom.

President Kennedy Reacts

When President Kennedy first heard about the march, he tried to get the black leaders to call it off. Kennedy was having trouble getting some of his ideas passed into law. Southerners in Congress didn't like Kennedy's Civil Rights Act. As long as Kennedy wanted to pass civil rights laws, these members of Congress wouldn't help him with other laws. For this reason, Kennedy thought that the march would attract too much attention to civil rights. He thought the march would make it harder for him to get other work done. Some white leaders in Congress thought that black people were going to make trouble for the country. However, once Kennedy saw that the march was really going to happen, he decided it would be better to support it than to fight it.

In the summer of 1963, civil rights leaders, including Martin Luther King Jr., met with President John F. Kennedy. The leaders wanted to make sure the president would support the march.

13

Different Groups Come Together

The march brought together many different kinds of **activists**. The leaders of the National Association for the Advancement of Colored People (NAACP) fought its battles in the courts. Other groups chose more direct methods. Groups like the Student Nonviolent Coordinating Committee (SNCC), an organization of college students, had many young members who were eager to challenge racists face to face. There were workers' groups, church groups, and other civil rights groups. Each had different ideas about how to fight **prejudice**. All were united in the idea of the march. Everyone worked hard to **compromise** to make it a peaceful march. Even on the day of the march, they were still struggling. John Lewis, a student leader, had written an angry speech. The other leaders talked him into finding a gentler way to say what he felt.

Leaders of six civil rights organizations met a month before the march. Left inset: Mrs. Medgar Evers, widow of a murdered civil rights worker, spoke to the NAACP. Right inset: Integration leaders met in New York.

SEGREGATION MUST GO NOW

Then and Now

As a young man in 1941, Bayard Rustin began working for the civil rights of others. He helped to plan the 1963 March on Washington, bringing together 250,000 people. This was the first of such marches on Washington.

Planning the March

With thousands of people planning to come to Washington, D.C., Bayard Rustin, a civil rights activist, was in charge of making sure that the march went smoothly. Rustin worked from a small office in Harlem, New York. He spent two months planning the events of the march. He arranged for special buses and trains to bring marchers into the city and to get them home. Rustin had drinking fountains and first-aid stations set up. Brown-bag lunches with sandwiches and fruit were made to be sold for 50 cents each. Rustin worked with the Washington, D.C., police and with the U.S. Army to provide security. Some shopkeepers were afraid that the march would become violent and that their goods would be stolen. There were thousands of police officers and soldiers on duty to make sure that everyone was safe.

March on Washington leader Bayard Rustin points to a map of the route the march would take. Inset: Rustin and marshals who were to guide marchers met at Friendship Baptist Church in New York's Harlem community.

All Together

Finally the day of the march arrived. It was August 28, 1963. During the early morning hours, 2,000 buses and dozens of trains brought people to the city for the march. Martin Luther King Jr. and the other leaders were scheduled to begin marching at 11:30 A.M. Some people couldn't wait quite that long. At 11:20 A.M., 10 minutes early, a high-school marching band, dressed in bright yellow silk jackets, started marching through the streets. More than 250,000 people followed. They were black and white, rich and poor, Hollywood stars and ordinary people. Famous singers such as Joan Baez and Bob Dylan performed onstage. Groups of schoolchildren clapped, danced, and sang **freedom songs** as the marchers passed by. They all believed that people should be treated fairly, no matter what color their skin was.

Marchers who gathered at the Lincoln Memorial cheered for the speakers. Inset: *Young people sang songs as they walked along Constitution Avenue in Washington, D.C.*

Martin Luther King Jr.'s Dream

The crowd marched through the streets of Washington, D.C., to the steps of the Lincoln Memorial. They gathered to hear the leaders of the Civil Rights movement speak. The speeches were about jobs, freedom, and laws. The leaders spoke about ways to make the country a better place for all Americans, black and white. Martin Luther King Jr. was known as a great speaker. That day he gave one of his most powerful speeches. He talked about his dream that one day all Americans would be able to live together in peace and to treat each other fairly. "I have a dream that one day, the sons of former slaves and the sons of former slave-owners will be able to sit down together at the table of brotherhood," said King. This speech would later be known as the "I Have a Dream" speech.

Martin Luther King Jr.'s speech lasted only about 16 minutes, but it was one of the most important speeches of the twentieth century.

The Dream Lives On

The 250,000 marchers were peaceful. The speeches were powerful. The march was the first demonstration to be organized entirely by black people. At the time, it was one of the biggest marches on Washington, D.C. It was one of the greatest moments of the Civil Rights movement. The march helped to show people around the country how important the goals of the movement were. It inspired many new people to join the struggle for civil rights. Kennedy's Civil Rights Act was passed into law. Since then, activists working for peace, for equal rights for women, and for many other interests have organized marches on Washington. They have followed in the footsteps of Martin Luther King Jr. and the marchers of 1963.

This picture shows the more than 250,000 people who crowded around the Lincoln Memorial to speak and to sing about jobs and freedom.

Glossary

activists (AK-tih-vists) People who take action for what they believe is right.

boycotts (BOY-kots) When a group of people agree to not buy a product or use a service in order to bring about change.

civil rights movement (SIH-vul RYTS MOOV-mint) People and groups working together to win freedom and equality for all people.

compromise (KOM-pruh-myz) When people give up part of what they want in order to come to an agreement.

defense industries (dih-FENS IN-dus-treez) Businesses that produce weapons and that supply them and other products to the military during wartime.

demonstrations (deh-mun-STRAY-shunz) Activities that people do to show how they feel about something.

freedom songs (FREE-dum SONGZ) Songs that civil rights activists sang to remind themselves and others that they were fighting for freedom.

Jim Crow laws (JIM KROH LAWZ) Laws that were created in the late 1800s by southern states to separate the races.

labor union (LAY-ber YOON-yun) A group of workers who organize to gain better wages and working conditions.

minimum wage (MIH-nih-mum WAYJ) The lowest wage that a worker can be legally paid.

prejudice (PREH-juh-dis) Disliking a group of people because they are different.

protests (PROH-tests) Events where activists demonstrate or speak out about something that they don't like.

racists (RAY-sists) People who believe that one group or race of people is better than another group or race.

segregation (seh-gruh-GAY-shun) The act of separating people of one race, gender, or social class from another.

Index

Primary Sources

Page 5 (left): "Father Carrying Daughter at March" on Washington. By Flip Schulke. **Page 5 (right)**: "Protester With a Backpack." By Wally McNamee. **Page 8**: A. Philip Randolph before statue at Lincoln Memorial. Library of Congress. **Page 11**: National headquarters in Harlem, New York, of the March on Washington. By O. Fernandez. Library of Congress. **Page 12**: "King Meeting With President Kennedy," Martin Luther King Jr. and civil rights leaders met with President John F. Kennedy and Vice President Lyndon B. Johnson. By Flip Schulke (August 1963). **Page 15**: Civil rights leaders—John Lewis; Whitney Young Jr.; A. Philip Randolph; Dr. Martin Luther King Jr.; James Farmer; and Roy Wilkins—met in New York City before the March on Washington. **Page 15 (right inset)**: Mrs. Medgar Evers spoke at NAACP rally at Howard University, a few days before the March on Washington. **Page 15 (left inset)**: Integration leaders planned strategy for the March (August 3, 1963). **Page 16**: Bayard Rustin, deputy director of the March on Washington maps march route. **Page 16 (inset)**: Bayard Rustin and March leaders met at Harlem's Friendship Baptist Church (August 13, 1963). **Page 19**: Marchers cheered Dr. King's Dream Speech. By Flip Schulke (August 28, 1963). **Page 19 (inset)**: Young people sang and chanted slogans at the start of the march. By Wally McNamee. **Page 20**: Dr. King delivered his "I Have a Dream" speech at the 1963 March on Washington. By Flip Schulke. **Page 22**: "March on Washington." By Flip Schulke (August 28, 1963).

Web Sites

Due to the changing nature of Internet links, PowerKids Press has developed an online list of Web sites related to the subject of this book. This site is updated regularly. Please use this link to access the list:

www.powerkidslinks.com/lcrm/1963mow/